SPANISH AMERICAN WAR

A History From Beginning to End

Copyright © 2016 by Hourly History Limited

Table of Contents

Introduction

A former U.S. ambassador to Great Britain once described the Spanish-American War as a "splendid little war", presumably because it lasted only ten weeks. Yet this "little war" arguably had one of the biggest impacts of any war on the configuration of global powers. U.S. history books might pay it little mind, but the Spanish-American War had significant consequences for the United States and the role it would come to play in world affairs. That, in turn, has had significant consequences for every other country in the world. Had it not been for this splendid little war, the United States might have remained isolationist in its foreign policy, which would have limited or at least delayed the attainment of its status as a superpower. Because of the Spanish-American War, however, the United States was thrust onto the global stage and began to have increasingly significant influence over international events.

The Spanish-American War also had significant consequences for numerous other countries. Spain, a once mighty superpower in its right, saw its global influence significantly reduced, but it also received economic benefits at the end of the war. Spaniards who had been living in the colonies came home and re-invested their money in Spain. Additionally, the U.S. paid Spain for the Philippines. This influx of money, combined with a reduction in the financial obligations necessary to maintain its colonies, allowed Spain to modernize its industries. Spanish poets, philosophers, and writers called for cultural changes as well. The result is that many modern Spaniards consider the war to have had a liberating effect on their country by allowing for a cultural revitalization accompanied by technological innovation and modernization.

Cuba, one of Spain's former colonies, was also significantly impacted. Cuba's struggle for independence had instigated the Spanish-American War, and although it was granted independence following the war, U.S. provisions in the Treaty of Paris and subsequent treaties with Cuba gave the U.S. considerable control over Cuban affairs. Therefore, despite its independent status, Cuba truly did not gain autonomy over its affairs for some time to come. The resentment that grew from U.S. manipulation of Cuban affairs spawned a number of violent interactions that ultimately resulted in the severing of ties between the two countries, a situation which only recently has begun to change.

The Philippines, like Cuba, had also been seeking independence from Spanish control. The revolution there had been quelled at the time of the Spanish-American War, but it was quickly revived when the U.S. offensive against Spain began. Despite the assistance of Filipino revolutionary forces during the war, the Philippines would not gain independence at the conclusion of hostilities, and another war, the Philippine-American War, began as a result. The U.S. would win this long and costly war, but the Philippines would eventually win their independence. This was not the case for the other two

Spanish colonies of Puerto Rico and Guam, both of which were annexed by the United States and remain U.S. Commonwealths in the present day.

Finally, this "little war" also impacted countries not directly involved in the hostilities. The outcome would continue to influence global events well into the future. When the U.S. was thrust onto the global stage, not all major superpowers were supportive. Germany took an aggressive stance against U.S. intervention, and while it backed down when conflict was threatened, there is an argument to be made that hostile exchanges set the stage for future events. The war also gave other countries a glimpse of how the United States would act as a player on the global stage. At home in the U.S., the American public now began to support an expansionist ideology as they saw themselves as righteous people fighting for righteous purposes. This shift in ideology continues to govern modern U.S. policy.

The Spanish-American War, therefore, despite its short duration, continues to impact the policies, economies, and ideologies of the various countries involved in the conflict. The consequences of the war have been far-reaching and historically significant. The international changes that occurred in the aftermath of the war can be argued to have had a significant impact on every country in the world, and *that* is the quintessential definition of a "splendid little war."

Chapter One

Prelude to War

"War should never be entered upon until every agency of peace has failed."

—President William McKinley

To understand any war, it is important to understand the context in which the decision to wage war was made. In the case of the Spanish-American War of 1898, the context was that of the Cuban War of Independence. Cuba had become a Spanish colony after the arrival of Columbus. Havana was briefly occupied by Britain in 1762 but was later exchanged with Spain for Florida. Spain utilized the island mainly as a harbor for the Spanish fleet as it gathered and transported New World riches back to the crown. In the nineteenth century, following the collapse of Haiti's sugar industry, the island became a major sugar producer. This had several effects, including sugar supplanting tobacco as the major agricultural crop, the arrival of increasing numbers of slaves needed for labor, and a change from poverty to prosperity for most of Cuba's residents. The latter played a large role in keeping Cuba loyal to Spain when much of the rest of Latin America was breaking away.

Toward the end of the nineteenth century, however, loyalties began to change as Spain's increasing despotism and taxation, the growth of Cuban nationalism, and Creole rivalry with Spaniards for control fostered dissatisfaction with Spanish rule. The result was the Ten Years' War against Spain from 1868 to 1878, but it did not result in Cuban independence. It did, however, result in the devaluation of the sugar market, which subsequently prompted U.S. businessmen to become involved. Business interests in the U.S. began to monopolize the Cuban sugar market, and by 1894, 90% of Cuban exports went to the U.S. and 40% of Cuban imports came from the U.S. This effectively gave U.S. interests economic authority, and thereby acting authority, despite Spain's continued political control.

While U.S. business interests in Cuba were increasing, the Cuba Libre movement was also gaining momentum. The movement's leader, José Martí, established offices in Florida and New York for the purpose of buying and smuggling weapons. Additionally, the movement had mounted a large-scale propaganda campaign that generated sympathy among Protestant churches and Democratic farmers, although U.S. businesses called on Washington to ignore pleas for support of the movement. Still, the stage was set for a revolution, and despite the lack of support by business interests, after years of organizing, José Martí launched a three-prong invasion of the island in 1895.

The invasion was to include a group from Santo Domingo, a group from Costa Rica, and one from the

U.S.. with this final contingent part of what was known as the Fernandina Plan. It called for forces to leave from Fernandina, Florida, pick up Costa Rican collaborator José Maceo Grajales, and head to Cuba to initiate the revolution with Máximo Gómez, who would be leading the Santo Domingo contingent. The U.S. government however detained the three ships that were part of the plan in Fernandina and confiscated the arms and supplies meant for the rebels. As a result, the initial impact of the invasion, while successful in provoking a revolutionary uprising, was not the show of force for which Martí had hoped. It quickly became evident that a protracted military campaign could not be avoided.

Spain's response, under the leadership of General Valeriano Weyler (who had been appointed to replace General Arsenio Martínez-Campos), was a variation of a tactic used extensively in other parts of the New World throughout Spain's occupation. Weyler sought to quell the revolution by depriving the rebels with necessary supplies and assistance. He did so by ordering the relocation of certain Cuban residents to what were called reconcentration areas. Spain had used a variation of this tactic successfully in other parts of the New World, such as in Peru where natives were forced to relocate to planned settlements called *reducciones* (singular *reducción*). The tactic can effectively prevent or slow insurgencies by relocating so-called troublemakers to communities of loyalists or to areas near military headquarters as was the case in Cuba. It did effectively slow the revolution, but it also fuelled the anti-Spain propaganda in the United States. In fact, when President William McKinley referred to the tactic as being uncivilized, he went so far as to call it "extermination."

Other political forces in the United States were influencing the situation as well. Theodore Roosevelt, who was Assistant Secretary of the Navy from 1897-1898, was an aggressive supporter of a war with Spain. He much admired Captain Alfred Thayer Mahan's theories regarding the role of naval strength in creating the world's dominant powers by securing international markets. He believed Cuba would be strategically important for U.S. naval domination. Additionally, he supported the liberation of the Cuban people, and he believed the Monroe Doctrine applied in this situation and should be upheld. A U.S. foreign policy established in 1823 by President James Monroe, the doctrine stated that any interference, including attempts to colonize land, by European nations in the Americas would be viewed by the U.S. as an act of aggression and one that would prompt U.S. intervention. It further stated that the U.S. would not interfere with existing colonies nor would it intervene in internal matters in European countries. Roosevelt believed, however, that, in accordance with the Monroe Doctrine, the United States could intervene in existing colonies in order to stabilize their economic affairs, particularly if those economic affairs affected U.S. business interests. This is a policy he would later formalize as President with an amendment to the Monroe Doctrine that came to be known as the Roosevelt Corollary. Given that the revolution and Spain's response were destabilizing the island nation's economy and impacting U.S. business interests, Roosevelt argued the U.S. had the right to intervene.

Among the U.S. businesses affected by the revolution were shipping firms that relied heavily on trade with Cuba and that had suffered losses as a result of the revolt. They pressured Congress and President McKinley to seek an end to the revolution. Investors in Cuban sugar also suffered losses, but they reached out to Spain to resolve the situation. From the American public's point of view, support for intervention was fostered by a comparison with America's own revolutionary history, at that time only a little over a century old. Furthermore, U.S. attempts to peacefully resolve the situation through mediation of negotiations between Spain's government and the rebels were met with rejection, first by the Spanish, who promised to give Cubans more autonomy but failed to deliver on that promise. Then, the rebels themselves rejected negotiations after a new, more liberal government in Spain offered to change the reconcentration policies in exchange for a cessation of hostilities.

In a further attempt to mitigate the hostilities, the liberal Spanish government recalled Governor General Valeriano Weyler. However, this action alarmed Cubans loyal to Spain, who then planned a demonstration upon the arrival of the new Governor General, Ramon Blanco. U.S. Consul Fitzhugh Lee learned about these demonstration plans and requested that a U.S. warship be dispatched to Cuba. The U.S. State Department dispatched the USS Maine. While docked in Havana Harbor, a massive explosion sunk the Maine, and with it, hopes of a negotiated peace.

Chapter Two

First Blood

"In peace, sons bury their fathers. In war, fathers bury their sons."

—Herodotus

When President McKinley sent the USS Maine to Havana Harbor to protect American citizens and interests, he also moved a large part of the North Atlantic Squadron to Key West and the Gulf of Mexico in preparation for the possibility that war could not be avoided. When the USS Maine was sunk by a massive explosion in Havana Harbor, that possibility became a reality. The USS Maine sank at 9:40 pm on February 15, 1898, and of the 355 sailors on board, 266 were killed. Fuelled by what many consider overly inflammatory or yellow journalism by leading journalists of the time such as Joseph Pulitzer and William Randolph Hearst, both of whom immediately blamed Spain for the explosion, the American public now became fully focused on the situation. Hearst and Pulitzer had been stoking the fires of anti-Spanish sentiment for some time, but since their papers only circulated in New York City and not nationally, recent scholars consider their impact to have been minimal outside of New York. After the sinking of the USS Maine, however, the entire nation started paying attention to what was going on in

Cuba. While many people had previously considered Spain simply a backward nation that was incapable of dealing with Cuba properly, they now saw a more serious threat.

Although President McKinley, like most American leaders, urged patience until the cause of the explosion could be determined, he also asked Congress to appropriate 50 million dollars for defense. Congress unanimously granted the request, and it soon became evident that a diplomatic solution to the conflict was not likely. Spain appealed to the European powers, but most of those supported the U.S. and urged Spain to give in and accept American terms. Germany was an exception, urging a united European stand against the U.S. instead, but it took no action related to that.

On March 28, the U.S. Navy issued the results of their investigation into the explosion that sank the Maine. The investigation concluded that the ship's powder magazines were ignited by an external explosion set off under the hull. This further fuelled American indignation and made war inevitable. Subsequent studies of the explosion at the time and well into the future have yielded contradictory results. Two relatively recent studies, one in 1974 conducted by General Hyman George Rickover and another by National Geographic in 1999, also came to contradictory conclusions. Rickover's team found the cause of the explosion to be internal while the National Geographic study found that, despite a lack of definitive evidence, the explosion could have been caused by a mine. None of these subsequent studies altered the outcome.

The U.S. Congress rapidly approved a joint resolution that authorized President McKinley to use military force as necessary to help Cuba gain independence. The resolution included the Teller Amendment, named after Colorado Senator Henry M. Teller, abdicating any U.S. intention to annex Cuba after the war. This amendment would later impact peace negotiations. President McKinley signed the resolution on April 20, 1898, and began a blockade of Cuba on April 21. Spain severed ties with the U.S. and declared war on April 23. On April 25, the U.S. Congress declared that a state of war had existed as of April 21, the date the blockade began. While the U.S. Navy was well-prepared to go to war, the army needed to make radical changes that included buying new supplies and enlisting at least 50,000 new men. This proved not to be a problem; American outrage, stoked by shouts of "Remember the Maine", translated into willing volunteers. The Army received over 220,000 new men through volunteers and National Guard unit mobilization.

Chapter Three

The Pacific Theatre

"War! That mad game the world so loves to play."

—Jonathan Swift

When President McKinley moved portions of the North Atlantic Squadron to Key West and the Gulf of Mexico and sent the USS Maine to Havana Harbor, he also moved forces into place just off Lisbon and Hong Kong. Because of the extent of Spanish territories, McKinley anticipated the need to attack Spain in locations outside of Cuba in the event that war ensured. In the Pacific, the two major Spanish colonies were the Philippines and Guam. Both had first been contacted by Europeans in 1521 when the Portuguese explorer Ferdinand Magellan, sailing under the Spanish flag, arrived in Guam on March 6 and in the Philippines on March 16 of that same year. Spain didn't claim these areas as colonies, however, until 1565 at the time of Miguel Lopez de Legazpi's expedition to the region. At that time, Lopez de Legazpi established the first permanent settlement of Cebu in the Philippines. Guam, on the other hand, while claimed by the Spanish as a colony during Legazpi's expedition, was not physically colonized until 1668 when Jesuit missionaries arrived to introduce Christianity and begin to develop trade.

At the time of the Spanish-American War, the Philippines had been embroiled in its own battle for independence from Spain. When U.S. troops arrived in the area, the revolution was in a state of truce after the signing of the Pact of Biak-na-Bato in 1897. The revolution's leaders had been exiled. While he had nothing to do with the planning or conducting of the revolt, José Rizal, whose writings inspired the revolution and is now considered one of the greatest heroes of the Philippines, was executed in 1896 by the Spanish for the crime of rebellion as a result of the revolution. Thus, the political situation in the Philippines, while subdued for the moment, was still unsettled when U.S. troops arrived in the area. This would prove to be useful to the American objectives.

The American forces in the Philippines consisted of the Asiatic Squadron commanded by Commodore George Dewey aboard the USS Olympia. The squadron was hampered by the fact that, after the Germans had seized the eastern Chinese port city of Tsingtao in 1897, it was the only naval force in the region without a local base. This caused coal and ammunition problems, but these proved not to be major obstacles. In the first battle between the Spanish and American forces, which took place in Manila Bay on May 1, the Asiatic Squadron was able to defeat the Spanish fleet in a matter of hours with only nine wounded. They successfully captured the harbor of Manila, and following their victory, warships from Germany, Britain, France, and Japan entered Manila Bay. Only the Germans acted aggressively, ignoring naval courtesy by refusing to salute the U.S. flag and cutting in front of U.S. ships. Additionally, they took soundings of the harbor and brought supplies to the besieged Spanish. When the Americans threatened conflict if the behavior continued, the Germans discontinued their provocative activities.

Commodore Dewey then brought one of the exiled revolutionary leaders, Emilio Aguinaldo, back from China, where he had been living. Working collaboratively, the Filipinos, under Aguinaldo's leadership, and the Americans under Dewey's command, were able to capture most of the islands by June. Aguinaldo proclaimed the independence of the Philippines on June 12, 1898, though much fighting remained to make that a reality. Unfortunately, a few months later in August, a group of American leaders who were unaware a cease-fire between Spain and the U.S. had just been signed took control of the city of Manila in the Battle of Manila. They prevented Filipino forces from entering the captured city, an act that the Filipinos deeply resented. It ended the collaborative efforts between the Americans and the Filipinos and led to the Philippine-American War from 1899-1902. Despite this, the American-Filipino collaboration was able to defeat the Spanish successfully, giving American forces full control of the Philippines on August 13, 1898.

While the battle in the Philippines encountered some complications, the American capture of Guam proceeded much more smoothly. A U.S. naval fleet consisting of the USS Charleston and three transport ships carrying U.S. troops to the Philippines, all of which were under the command of Captain Henry Glass, entered Guam's Apra Harbor on June 20, 1898. Glass had received orders to capture Guam, and upon entering the harbor, fired cannon rounds at Fort Santa Cruz. They were puzzled when no one returned fire. Two local officials then came out to the Charleston and apologized to the Captain for being unable to return his cannon salute because they were out of gunpowder. Captain Glass informed them at that time that the U.S. and Spain were at war, something of which they were not aware. The following day, the surrender of the Spanish garrison and the island was arranged, and 54 Spanish infantrymen were captured and held as prisoners of war. Glass decided not to leave any troops on the island. Instead, Frank Portusach, who was the only American citizen on the island at the time of its capture, agreed to look after things until the fleet could return.

Chapter Four

The Caribbean Theatre

"I should welcome almost any war for I think this country needs one."

—Theodore Roosevelt

Theodore Roosevelt was long a proponent of war with Spain, and in his role as Assistant Secretary of the Navy, he was instrumental in preparing the U.S. for war. He appointed George Dewey as the commander of the Asiatic Squadron, helped ready the U.S. Navy for war, and along with Leonard Wood, convinced the army to raise the 1st U.S. Volunteer Cavalry, which under Wood's command quickly came to be known as the "Rough Riders." Roosevelt himself would ride with the Rough Riders, and as a result is recognized as one of the heroes of this war. He was an integral part of planning U.S. strategy, which in the Caribbean involved land and sea campaigns in both Cuba and Puerto Rico.

The land campaign in Cuba involved the capture of the city of Santiago de Cuba, but the effort for this was not without its difficulties. In order to capture the city, U.S. troops would have first to get through Spanish strongholds in the San Juan Hills and the town of El Caney. On June 22, the Fifth Army Corps, commanded by General William R. Shafter, landed at Daiquirí and

Siboney located to the east of Santiago. A few days later, an engagement with Spanish troops saw the Spanish retreat to their lightly entrenched positions in Las Guasimas. An advance guard, under the command of General Joseph Wheeler, was sent to engage the Spanish contingent. They employed more traditional linear tactics while the Spanish utilized tactics of cover and concealment which they had learned from their skirmishes with the Cuban rebels. The Spanish ambushed the American forces and were successfully able to defeat them in the Battle of Las Guasimas on June 24. This showed American commanders that they couldn't stick to the traditional linear warfare model when engaging the Spanish. They began to use similar tactics of concealment and found more success as a result.

On July 1, a combined force of some 15,000 U.S. troops, including Teddy Roosevelt and the Rough Riders, advanced on entrenched Spaniards at the Battle of El Caney and the Battle of San Juan Hill near Santiago. The Americans were victorious in these battles; however, 200 U.S. soldiers were killed and 1,200 were wounded thanks to a high rate of down range fire the Spanish were able to employ. Despite initial U.S. success, however, the Spanish were ultimately able to defend Fort Canosa and halt the American land advancement into Santiago. The Americans fought on, slowly advancing on the Spanish position, but heat exhaustion and mosquito-borne disease took their toll. Meanwhile, rebel forces led by Calixto Garcia were advancing on the city from the west. Garcia had also aided the invasion effort by securing the landing places for the Army, and he supported the U.S. Marines in their invasion of Guantánamo when they had problems with the Spanish guerrilla tactics. Furthermore, by the time of the American landing, he had already secured the interior of the old Oriente Province using mobile artillery. Though he was a valuable asset to the U.S. effort, when the Americans were successful in securing the city of Santiago, he was denied entrance.

While infantry troops were inching their way toward the city by land, the U.S. Navy was advancing on the city from the sea. The American Navy had been using Guantánamo Bay as shelter during the summer hurricane season after a successful invasion there which had taken place between June 6 and June 10. They had spotted the Spanish fleet, known as the Flota de Ultramar, commanded by Admiral Pascual Cervera y Topete, taking shelter in Santiago harbor. A two-month standoff ensued. On July 3, in the largest naval battle of the war, the Navy engaged with the Spanish fleet as they finally tried to leave the harbor. The battle that followed resulted in the U.S. forces grounding or sinking five of the six ships in the fleet. The one ship that survived the attack, the Cristóbal Colón, was ultimately scuttled by her captain when American forces caught up to her. The 1,612 Spanish sailors captured in the battle were transported to the U.S. and held as prisoners of war on Seavey's Island in Maine until mid-September. This group included Admiral Cervera. The decisive victory effectively spelled defeat for the Spanish forces in Cuba.

In Puerto Rico, U.S. forces also advanced by both land and sea, but the results were more mixed. The American offensive began by sea on May 12, 1898. Rear Admiral William T. Sampson, commanding 12 ships, attacked the capital of San Juan and was successfully able to establish a blockade of the city's harbor. Subsequent Spanish counterattacks were effectively repelled. The land offensive consisted of 1,300 infantry soldiers under the command of Nelson A. Miles. It began on July 25, and by August 1, after the Battle of Yauco and the Battle of Fajardo, the U.S. had taken control of Fajardo. A group of 200 Puerto Rican Spanish soldiers, under the command of Pedro del Pino, regained control of the city, however, forcing the withdrawal of American troops on August 5.

The Battle of Guayama and the Battle of Asomante were fought as U.S. troops advanced into the interior of the island. These battles were inconclusive however as larger and more effective Spanish opposition forced the retreat of U.S. troops. U.S. forces were more successful in the Battle of San Germán, causing the Spanish forces to retreat. On August 9, however, on a mountain known as Cerro Gervasio del Asomante, several U.S. soldiers were injured, and when the unit returned a few days later and attempted a surprise attack, five American commanders were gravely injured, prompting another retreat. On August 13, an armistice was signed whereby Spain relinquished its sovereignty over Puerto Rico. This act suspended all hostilities on the island.

Chapter Five

War's End

*"Beautiful the war and all its deeds of carnage must in time
be utterly lost,*

*That the hands of the sisters Death and Night incessantly
softly wash again, and ever again, this soil'd world;*

For my enemy is dead, a man as divine as myself is dead..."

—Walt Whitman

Spain sued for peace after suffering defeats in Cuba and
the Philippines and losing both of its fleets. Negotiations
began after a peace protocol was signed on August 12,
1898. Two months of difficult negotiations would follow.
In accordance with the terms of the protocol, both the
United States and Spain would appoint not more than five
commissioners to negotiate a treaty on their behalf. The
United States Commission was somewhat unusual in that
it included three senators. The reason this was considered
unusual was that they would then be voting on their own
negotiations when it came time to vote on the treaty. The
U.S. Commission consisted of William R. Day, a former
Secretary of State who had resigned his position in order
to lead the commission; William P. Frye, a senator from

Maine; Cushman Kellogg Davis, a senator from Minnesota; George Gray, a senator from Delaware; and Whitlaw Reid, a former diplomat and one-time vice presidential nominee. The Spanish commission consisted of five Spanish diplomats and one French diplomat. The Spanish diplomats were Eugenio Montero Rios, Buenaventura de Abarzuza, José de Garnica, Wenceslao Ramírez de Villa-Urrutia, and Rafael Cerero. The French diplomat was Jules Cambon. A Filipino lawyer, Felipe Agoncillo, was denied the right to participate in the negotiations on behalf of the Philippines.

Formal negotiations, which took place at the Ministry of Foreign Affairs in Paris, began on October 1, 1898. Things promptly got off to a rocky start when Spain demanded that Manila be returned to its authority because U.S. forces had captured it a few hours *after* the signing of the peace protocol in Washington. The U.S. refused to consider it, and for the moment, the issue was tabled. For almost the first month, the negotiations focused on Cuba. While the U.S. had annexed the Philippines, Puerto Rico, and Guam, the Teller Amendment, which was part of the U.S. declaration of war, made it impractical for America to do the same with Cuba. Spain initially refused to accept Cuba's national debt, which totaled 400 million dollars. Eventually, however, Spain had no choice and had to accept it. Cuba was granted to the Cubans, although the U.S. retained control over Guantánamo Bay, the situation of which was guaranteed by the Platt Amendment and ultimately formalized in the 1903 Cuban-American Treaty of

Relations. The treaty states the U.S. will have the right to exercise complete jurisdiction over the bay, even though Cuba retains sovereignty. The U.S. established a naval base at Guantánamo Bay and has occupied the territory ever since. The current Cuban government considers the U.S. occupation to be illegal and wants the territory to be returned. The naval base, and prisoner detention facility located there, has faced international criticism following the U.S. decision to detain, indefinitely, over 500 prisoners of the "War on Terror" following the terrorist attacks on the World Trade Center and the Pentagon on September 11, 2001.

As negotiations focused on other Spanish territories, Spain agreed to cede Guam and Puerto Rico to the United States. When the negotiations turned again to the Philippines however, Spain was not so conciliatory. Negotiators for Spain had hoped to be able to retain most of the territory in the Philippines, offering at first only to cede perhaps Mindanao and the Sulu Islands. The American commission had considered this offer as well as Chairman Day's suggestion that the U.S. only retain the naval base in Manila Bay as a local base of operations for the Asiatic Squadron. Others had only recommended retaining control of Luzon. The commission, acting on explicit instructions from President McKinley however, ultimately concluded that should Spain retain control over any territory in the Philippines, it would likely sell part or all of it to other European powers, which would eventually cause problems for the United States. President McKinley's cabled instructions read in part "...to accept merely Luzon, leaving the rest of the islands subject to Spanish rule, or to be the subject of future contention, cannot be justified on political, commercial, or humanitarian grounds." The possibility the negotiations would collapse, and that war would resume, grew with debate over this issue. When President McKinley's Republican majority was reduced after U.S. elections in November of that year, the delegation took notice and offered Spain money, 20 million dollars to be exact, in exchange for the islands. The offer was approximately one-tenth the estimated value of the Philippines and Spain's delegation reacted with angry indignation at the offer. The Queen-Regent Maria Christina, however, noting a lack of material means to defend Spain's rights and a desire to avoid the horrors of war, grudgingly accepted the offer. The Spanish legislature in Madrid rejected it, but the Queen-Regent had been granted authority to sign the treaty by Spain's constitution.

With the signing of the treaty and Spain's agreement despite legislative rejection, that left only U.S. ratification. In the U.S. Senate, four schools of thought influenced the debate regarding ratification. One group, consisting mainly of Republicans, generally supported the treaty, but a small faction of Republicans sought to defeat it as long as it contained the agreement for the acquisition of the Philippines. Still another group was against the treaty entirely. Among Democrats, most supported it and expansion in general, but a small group of Democrats argued for approval of the treaty to put an end to the war, after which the U.S. could grant independence to the Philippines as well as Cuba.

As the debate proceeded in the Senate, those opposing the treaty argued it cast the U.S. as an imperialist nation, something U.S. Senator George Frisbie Hoar called vulgar. Senators in favor of the treaty argued that not approving it would prevent the U.S. from taking its rightful place as a world power. Some also argued that it was the duty of the U.S. to extend the Christian civilization. Interestingly, those who argued for an expansionist approach also emphasized that the U.S. Constitution only applied to U.S. citizens and not to citizens of U.S. territories. Influential U.S. citizens also weighed in on the controversy. Mark Twain and Samuel Gompers opposed it based on its imperialist policies. Andrew Carnegie and former President Grover Cleveland also petitioned the Senate to reject it. Despite much controversy, the Treaty of Paris was finally approved on February 6, 1899. It received only one vote more than the two-thirds majority needed to pass; the vote was 57 – 27 in favor of passage.

The provisions of the treaty gave Cuba its independence from Spain, but the Platt Amendment made sure the U.S. would retain control of the island nation while it discharged the obligations that resulted from its occupation. The Platt Amendment laid out seven provisions that would have to be met before the U.S. would withdraw troops. The provisions in general limited Cuba's ability to conduct foreign policy including making treaties with other nations, gave the U.S. the power to intervene in Cuba's affairs, and pledged the lease of land for naval bases to the United States. Cuba was obliged as well to include the text of the Platt Amendment in its constitution. It wouldn't be until 1934 before most of the provisions of the Platt Amendment would be repealed.

Aside from Cuba, Spain also agreed to cede Puerto Rico and its other possessions in the West Indies to the United States as well as the island of Guam in the Pacific. The Philippines were to be surrendered for a payment of 20 million dollars. The U.S. paid an additional $100,000 to Spain in 1900 for a statement of clarification known as the Treaty of Washington. This statement sought to remove any misunderstanding regarding Spain's territorial holdings, and what it was therefore ceding to the United States in the Philippines. The Philippines were discussed in Article III of the Treaty of Paris, but the specifics concerning territorial boundaries were not described.

While the Treaty of Paris formally ended the Spanish-American War, it came with numerous consequences. It marked the beginning of the United States taking its role among the world powers. The attainment of Spanish territories also expanded the economic dominance of the United States, particularly in the Pacific. President McKinley's role in the treaty negotiations changed the role of the office of the President from what used to be a weak position to one which became the foundation for the much stronger position that currently exists. Additionally, the U.S. military occupation of numerous bases abroad had several long-term impacts. The war lasted ten weeks, but its impact changed the global power structure and shaped events long into the future, even to the present day.

Chapter Six

Consequences of War: The United States

"Let us ever remember that our interest is in concord, not in conflict; and that our real eminence rests in the victories of peace, not those of war."

—President William McKinley

When writing to his friend Theodore Roosevelt, John Hay, the U.S. Ambassador to the United Kingdom, called the Spanish-American War "a splendid little war." The war had only lasted ten weeks, but it had proved a uniting force for U.S. citizens, who were still stinging from the division the American Civil War had caused between the northern and southern states. Four Confederate (i.e., southern state) generals served in the Spanish-American war and carried similar ranks as they had in the Civil War. Joseph Wheeler was one of those, and was the only one among them who saw action. Still, their inclusion with their former ranks demonstrated the desire on the part of the victorious Northerners to unify the country.

The war, therefore, acted to heal the American psyche by redefining the national identity and helping to repair the social divisions that the long and bloody Civil War had created. America now had a common enemy.

Northerners and southerners, previously enemies, were now fighting side by side in this war. Many lasting friendships between former rivals were created as a result. Additionally, the African-American community, which had supported the rebels in Cuba and the U.S. entry into the war, fought and gained prestige for their performance in the U.S. armed forces. In fact, 33 African-American sailors died in the explosion on the Maine. Booker T. Washington, an influential leader in the African-American community, argued vigorously that his race was ready to fight in this war and eager to demonstrate their loyalty to the United States. He saw the sacrifice of black lives as a means to gain ultimately freedom and rights for African-Americans, as the broader American community would witness their valor and patriotism.

Certainly, the American public loves their war heroes. Many individuals benefitted from their role in the war, not the least of which was Theodore Roosevelt. For him, it was indeed a "splendid little war" as he returned home a hero and was soon elected governor of New York. He became William McKinley's Vice President during his successful presidential re-election bid in 1900; and very quickly after that, Roosevelt became the 26th President of the United States following McKinley's assassination in September of 1900. Roosevelt was then re-elected in 1904 to a second term. He is still thought of as one of America's most beloved, successful, and colorful presidents.

The war changed not only the way the world viewed the United States but how the United States thought of itself as well. Following the war, the U.S. became a world power, and since that time it has played a significant role in conflicts around the world, whether by supporting other countries passively, by actively fighting in those conflicts, or by mediating peace negotiations. The war proved to the world that the U.S. was fully capable of defending its boundaries, its principles, and its neighbors. It also showed to the world that the U.S. was willing to intervene, and could do so successfully, in the affairs of other nations. Thus, the Spanish-American War marks the entry of the United States onto the global stage, both as a military and economic force.

It was not just the world that saw a different America; its citizens also changed the way they saw their country. Americans began to see themselves as a righteous people in service of a righteous purpose, namely the defending of democracy. This ideal would play a significant role in many wars to come. Americans also began to think differently about American imperialism or expansionism, the latter being the term that supporters preferred. Where before it was something the majority of the American public was against, many people now adopted the view that expansionism had its place, particularly as it assisted that righteous purpose. Of course, it had its economic benefits that bolstered support as well.

Economic downturns earlier in the 1890s had led to a U.S. depression known as the Panic of 1893. U.S. investments in Argentina suffered after the failure of the 1890 wheat crop and a coup in Buenos Aires. Fears among European investors led to a run on U.S. gold. This eventually led to a run on the banks, a credit crunch, and a sell-off of American stocks. By the time the dust settled, 500 banks had closed, 15,000 businesses had failed, and numerous farms had gone out of business. The American public blamed the Democrats, led by President Grover Cleveland, and in the elections of 1894, they handed the Republicans what remains the largest Republican political gains in U.S. history. This included electing William McKinley, Jr., as the 25th U.S. President.

The depression highlighted the threat posed by ignoring international problems that could affect American businesses, something that Theodore Roosevelt argued could justify U.S. intervention in the affairs of its neighbors. The American public now saw that the isolationist foreign policy that had prevailed for years could have severe consequences. A State Department memorandum issued in 1898 officially recognized that it was ill-advised to ignore problems abroad. It stated, "we can no longer afford to disregard international rivalries now that we ourselves have become a competitor in the world-wide struggle for trade." These concerns, coupled with the success of the Spanish-American War, laid the foundation for the marriage between U.S. foreign policy and business interests that prevail to the present day.

While it was a short-lived war, it could be argued that the consequences of this "splendid little war" for the United States had a major impact on U.S. history. It reunited a deeply divided country after a bitter and costly civil war. It catapulted the United States onto the world stage, where it now was seen as a major international power. It caused a reversal of U.S. isolationist policy to one of expansionism, and that resulted in the current union of U.S. foreign policy with business interests. It also changed the fortunes of individuals such as Teddy Roosevelt, who went on to have a highly successful political career. Finally, it marked the symbolic re-categorization of recently liberated slaves as American citizens with all that entails, including the responsibility of defending and perhaps dying for their country. Although they still presently struggle with the legacy of slavery and racism, African-American participation in the Spanish-American War was an early step toward taking their rightful place in American society and history.

Chapter Seven

Consequences of War: Spain

"Peace hath her victories, no less renowned than War."

—John Milton

For Spain, defeat in the Spanish-American War brought a significant reduction in the size of the empire. At the end of the war, Spain only retained a few international holdings. These included Spanish Morocco, Spanish West Africa, Spanish Guinea, and the Canary Islands. Thus, the loss of the war resulted in Spain's further decline as an imperial power, something which had begun with Napoleon's invasion in the early 19th century, which had resulted in the Peninsular War from 1808-1814. The duration and intensity of that war destroyed Spain's economic, political, and social structure. The old social order in Spain did not survive, and its culture was significantly altered. The void created by the conflict and its aftermath ignited a search for a new identity, and it was during this time that many of Spain's holdings in the Americas fought for and won their independence. By 1824, 16 republics had gained their independence from Spain. Spaniards had a particular affinity for Cuba however, considering it a province of Spain rather than simply a colony. Additionally, Spanish loyalists fleeing the newly created independent republics in the New World took refuge in Cuba. For these reasons, it wasn't until later in the century that Cubans initiated their war for independence, which set the stage for the Spanish-American War.

Because of the affinity that Spaniards held for Cuba, the loss of that colony after the Spanish-American War created a national trauma for Spain. In the wake of that trauma, a group of novelists, poets, and philosophers formed what came to be known as the Generation of '98. They heavily criticized Spain's literary and educational establishments, and their resistance to the restoration movement that occurred after the war helped to spark a renaissance movement in Spanish culture. They opposed the restoration of the monarchy, revived Spanish myths, brought back traditional and lost words, and supported the idea of Spanish regionalism, which would guarantee limited autonomy to the many nationalities and regions within Spain. Their influence would be far-reaching, eventually leading to the decentralized unitary state found in Spain today, which is composed of 17 autonomous communities.

Spain also benefitted economically in the aftermath of the war when large sums of money held by Spaniards in Cuba and America were re-invested in Spain. Additionally, there were the 20 million dollars the U.S. paid for the Philippines and a further $100,000 paid for the Treaty of Washington clarification statement in 1900. Spain used the influx of capital to create large, modern firms in the financial, steel, mechanical, chemical, textile, shipyard, and electric power industries.

While Spain lost the majority of its colonies and saw a reduction in its global influence, the cultural struggles that began early in the 19th century intensified and became clarified as a result of the Spanish-American War and its outcome. That ultimately led to a complete reorganization of Spain's political, cultural, and social structure. Many modern Spaniards consider that the war ultimately liberated Spain from an imperialist ideology that had long stifled modernization and cultural development. Losing the war, then, allowed Spain to renovate its cultural ideals and focus, for the first time, in the future and its continued development in a modern world.

Chapter Eight

Consequences of War: Cuba

"One is left with the horrible feeling now that war settles nothing; that to win a war is as disastrous as to lose one."

—Agatha Christie

For Cuba, whose struggle for independence had ultimately ignited the Spanish-American War, the outcome was far less successful than initially hoped. While the Teller Amendment prevented the U.S. from annexing Cuba outright, the Platt Amendment and subsequent Cuban-American Treaty of Relations guaranteed that the U.S. would retain a significant amount of control over Cuba's activities. The Platt Amendment prevented Cuba from signing treaties with other nations and contracting a national debt. The Cuban-American Treaty of Relations established a permanent U.S. military base at Guantánamo Bay. Thus, despite having gained independence, Cubans had not truly gained autonomy over their own affairs. Cuba officially gained independence in 1902 after all of the various treaties and provisions following the Spanish-American War had been approved and fulfilled. Because of the five years of U.S. military occupation following the war, Cuba suffered fewer problems when it finally emerged as an independent nation. Prosperity had increased during the early years following the war, and social tensions were not high.

As time went on, however, corruption, violence, and political irresponsibility provoked U.S. military intervention in 1906, 1917, and 1921. Additionally, America's economic involvement began to weaken Cuba's growth as a nation and fostered an increasing dependence on the United States. In the 1930s, the cruel dictatorship of Gerardo Machado y Morales, the worldwide economic depression, and growth in control over Cuba's economy by Spanish and North American interests provoked Cuban students and intellectuals to seek radical reforms. Machado was forced to flee the country on August 12, 1933. The U.S.-backed regime of Carlos Manuel de Céspedes assumed control; however, in what became known as the Sergeant's Revolt, Sergeant Fulgencio Batista y Zaldívar joined forces with militant students and took control from Céspedes on September 4. This was a turning point in Cuban history that ultimately resulted in the emergence of the military as arbiters of Cuban politics and culminated in the election of Batista as President in 1940.

Batista's early rule came to an end during World War II. This was followed by an era of prosperity in the post-war years. This period of growth and peace ended as political corruption and violence again increased, ultimately coming to a head with Batista staging a coup d'état and seizing power again in 1952. Cuba then entered a chaotic period of dictatorship, social polarization, and civil war that ended in the destruction of the military and most Cuban institutions. This period saw the rise of a charismatic leader, Fidel Castro, who seized power on January 1, 1959. He subsequently expropriated U.S. properties and investments and converted Cuba to a communist system. U.S.-Cuba relations deteriorated rapidly; diplomatic relations were severed on January 3, 1961, following a U.S. imposed embargo on Cuba in 1960. The embargo persists to the present day. Only recently has the U.S. ended its policy of isolation toward Cuba, which has resulted in relaxed travel restrictions and lessened bans on economic activity. Additionally, both countries have re-opened embassies in Washington and Havana. U.S. President Barack Obama has also called for lifting the embargo, although that has yet to occur.

The legacy of the Spanish-American War for Cuba, therefore, can perhaps best be described as a rocky road toward true independence. U.S. imposed restrictions, and continued intervention in Cuban affairs following the war, led to a chaotic cycle of dictatorship and revolution as Cuba has sought to foster its own economic growth and find a political structure that suits its people. U.S. policy toward Cuba fostered resentment that ultimately led to the expulsion of U.S. business interests and the expropriation of U.S. investments when Cuba was finally able to gain full autonomy over its own affairs. There is also an argument to be made that U.S. manipulation of Cuban affairs led to the political choices that ultimately resulted in the full erosion of U.S.-Cuba relations, relations that have yet to be fully re-established even after more than 50 years.

Chapter Nine

Consequences of War: The Philippines

"Wars are poor chisels for carving out peaceful tomorrows."

—Martin Luther King, Jr.

The aftermath of the Spanish-American War in the Philippines was significant. While Filipino revolutionaries had collaborated with U.S. forces to wrest control of the islands from the Spanish, the Filipino goal was full independence. Resentment for U.S. occupation began when American forces refused to allow Filipinos access to the city of Manila. Conflict erupted when the First Philippine Republic objected to U.S. forces taking possession of the Philippines under the terms of the Treaty of Paris. A Filipino lawyer, Felipe Agoncillo, had not been allowed to participate in the treaty negotiations on behalf of the Philippines. Armed conflict began on February 4, 1899, with the Second Battle of Manila. The battle was fought between 19,000 Americans and 15,000 Filipinos. It was instigated when American forces, who had been ordered to turn away insurgents from their encampment, fired upon Filipinos who were encroaching upon the American position. Attempts at a brokered ceasefire by Philippine President and ex-revolutionary leader Emilio Aguinaldo were rejected by American General Elwell Stephen Otis. The fighting escalated, but ended the next day with an American victory. Filipino resentment grew, however, and the First Philippine Republic officially declared war against the United States on June 2, 1899.

The war ended on July 2, 1902, with an American victory. It was, however, a much bloodier and much more costly war for the U.S. than the Spanish-American War had been; despite the official end of the war in 1902, Philippine revolutionaries would continue to battle U.S. forces occupying the islands. Those hostilities would not end until the Battle of Bud Bagsak on June 15, 1913. The war and subsequent U.S. occupation of the islands significantly changed the Philippine culture, one that would become particularly vulnerable following the significant reduction in population that resulted from the fighting as well as the disease and hunger that followed the conflict. An estimated 34,000 to 220,000 Filipinos died as a result of the war. Additionally, the U.S. "disestablished" the Catholic Church as the state church and introduced English as the primary language of government, education, and business. As had also occurred when these tactics were used among Native American populations in the U.S., the culture of the Philippines was forever altered.

In 1902, the U.S. did grant limited self-government for Filipinos, which included the right to vote for some elected officials. In 1916, the Philippine Autonomy Act was passed by the U.S. Congress under the Presidency of

Woodrow Wilson. The act promised eventual independence, and in the meantime, it established more Filipino control over their own affairs. The Philippine Independence Act of 1934 granted a limited form of independence with the promise of full independence by 1944. World War II, however, would interrupt the process and delay full independence until 1946 after the end of the Japanese occupation of the islands. Full independence was granted by the Treaty of Manila, which contained agreements regarding friendly relations with the U.S. that included diplomatic and consular representation.

In sum, the Spanish-American War and its aftermath in the Philippines provoked yet another war with the U.S., one that would be much longer, costlier, and bloodier. That conflict would be followed by a lengthy U.S. occupation before the Philippines would be granted their long-awaited independence.

Chapter Ten

Consequences of War: Puerto Rico and Guam

"To the victor belong the spoils."

—Senator William L. Marcy

Along with the Philippines, the U.S. annexed Puerto Rico and Guam following the Spanish-American War. U.S. occupation of Puerto Rico had significant economic impacts. The sugar industry in Puerto Rico had been in decline before the war due to the need for costly technological advances that were implemented in the latter half of the 19th century that became crucial in order to remain competitive in the industry. As a result, at the time of the war, there had been an agricultural shift toward coffee production. After the war, however, U.S. occupation reversed those trends. U.S.-instituted business policies made it harder for local farmers to stay in business while at the same time making it easier for American businesses to accumulate land. U.S. business investment subsequently led to a resurgence in the sugar industry. The inclusion of Puerto Rico in the U.S. tariff system as a customs area resulted in state-like status for the territory and benefitted the sugar exports through tariff protection.

Coffee was not protected under this system, and furthermore, since Puerto Rico and Cuba were no longer Spanish territories, both Cuba and Spain began to subject Puerto Rico to previously non-existent import tariffs. Thus, once again, sugar and coffee traded places in the Puerto Rican economy with sugar exports to the U.S. soaring; meanwhile, coffee exports went from 65.8% to a mere 19.6% between the years of 1897 and 1901. Tobacco was protected by the tariff system, however, and as a result, it grew from a nearly non-existent industry to a major part of the agricultural economy.

Politically, the first 20 years of U.S. occupation in Puerto Rico saw numerous attempts to obtain more democratic rights from the United States. In 1900, the Foraker Act established a civil government, and in 1917, the Jones Act gave Puerto Ricans U.S. citizenship. That prompted the drafting of Puerto Rico's Constitution, which was approved by voters, both U.S. and Puerto Rican, in 1952. The political status of Puerto Rico, however, remains as a Commonwealth controlled by the United States; modern relations between the U.S. and Puerto Rico have been strained due to economic policies towards Puerto Rico that have been characterized by many as colonialist and imperialistic.

Guam also saw numerous changes with U.S. occupation. Immediately following the end of the war, it became part of the U.S. telegraph line to the Philippines and a way station for U.S. ships traveling to and from the Philippines. It also served as an important naval base for the United States. During World War II, Guam was captured and occupied by Japanese forces between 1941 and 1944. When the U.S. recaptured Guam in August of 1944, it once again became an operations base for the U.S. Navy and Air Force. With the U.S. once more asserting itself in the affairs of Guam, resentment began to build on the part of the native Chamorro leaders, and they began to seek greater autonomy. The Guam Organic Act of 1950 established the island as an organized territory of the United States. That allowed Guam to establish a civilian government. Following that, the Immigration and Nationality Act of 1952 gave U.S. citizenship to all persons born on Guam on or after April 11, 1899. A series of laws that followed allowed Guam to elect their own governor and granted the island a delegate in the U.S. House of Representatives, although that delegate it not allowed a vote on the floor of the House.

After a series of attempts to address options for self-determination and decolonization, voters on Guam were given a choice in 1982 between statehood and becoming a Commonwealth of the United States. The latter would establish a closer relationship with the U.S. Voters could also opt to remain an unincorporated territory. After the initial vote and a runoff election, voters of Guam chose to become a Commonwealth, and it continues to be a strategically vital military installation for the U.S. in the Pacific Ocean.

Conclusion

The Spanish-American War was fought over the course of ten weeks between April 21 and August 12, 1898. Despite what its short duration might suggest, many of the battles were bloody and difficult to win. Ultimately, battles fought on numerous fronts likely affected the outcome for Spain. Not only was Spain at war with the U.S., but it also had to contend with revolutionary forces in both Cuba and the Philippines. Previous wars and significant cultural shifts had already had a major impact on Spain's ability to maintain control of its colonies and weakened its response to conflict. With U.S. intervention on behalf of Cuban revolutionaries, the outcome was almost inevitable, though that did not make the battles any easier. U.S. naval domination played a significant role in securing a victory. While land forces often struggled to hold or advance the line, the U.S. Navy was decisively victorious in each of its major battles. The flexible strategy of U.S. commanders allowed the forces to respond effectively to the tactics of the experienced Spanish fighters. The defeat of the Spanish fleets in both the Caribbean and the Pacific brought hostilities to an end, and peace negotiations ensued.

While the Spanish-American war was short in duration, it was long in aftermath. Peace negotiations took longer to produce and approve an accord than the war itself. Once approved, however, the conclusion of the war brought numerous changes. One change, the change in the status of super powers, saw the rise of the United States and the decline of Spain. For Spain, this had beneficial economic effects and brought about both cultural revitalization and technological modernization. The U.S., for its part, would begin to play an increasingly important role in international affairs. A change in the ideology of the American public would foster U.S. intervention in numerous conflicts to come. Cuba would gain independence though not full autonomy, and this would foster resentment that provoked numerous violent internal political shifts, until at last, Cuba would fully gain autonomy, become a Communist nation, and promptly sever all ties with the United States. The frosty relations and the consequences that followed included, among other problems, a nuclear crisis known as the Bay of Pigs Incident, or the Cuban Missile Crisis. While nuclear war was averted, relations between Cuba and the United States are only now beginning to thaw.

For the other former colonies of Spain, the war had mixed results. The Philippines, which had been seeking independence at the time of the Spanish-American War, was denied it upon cessation of hostilities. This provoked another war, the Philippine-American War, and while the U.S. was victorious, it was a longer and costlier conflict. As a result of war and U.S. occupation, the population of the islands was significantly reduced and the culture of the Philippine inhabitants was forever changed. The Philippines would eventually gain their independence, but the question remains, at what cost?

Puerto Rico and Guam were both annexed by the United States and both remain U.S. Commonwealths today. Both also struggled with the question of autonomy, but since the inhabitants of each were given U.S. citizenship rights, there has been little movement towards independence. Guam, in fact, elected to remain a U.S. Commonwealth rather than choosing independent statehood.

Another important consequence of the war was the role it played in the economies of the various participants. Spain, Puerto Rico, and Guam would see economic benefits from the end of the war whereas the results were more mixed for Cuba. The U.S. benefitted economically and strategically by securing naval bases in both the Pacific and the Caribbean, just as Theodore Roosevelt and Captain Alfred Thayer Mahan would have predicted. All in all, the impact of this so-called "splendid little war" was not always splendid and not at all little.

Made in the USA
San Bernardino, CA
21 February 2020